Backyard Bird Watchers

A Bird Watcher's Guide to

MOCKINGBIRDS

By
Aife Arnim

Gareth Stevens
PUBLISHING

Please visit our website, www.garethstevens.com. For a free color catalog of all our high-quality books, call toll free 1-800-542-2595 or fax 1-877-542-2596.

Cataloging-in-Publication Data

Names: Arnim, Aife.
Title: A bird watcher's guide to mockingbirds / Aife Arnim.
Description: New York : Gareth Stevens Publishing, 2018. | Series: Backyard Bird Watchers | Includes index.
Identifiers: ISBN 9781538203194 (pbk.) | ISBN 9781538203217 (library bound) | ISBN 9781538203200 (6 pack)
Subjects: LCSH: Mockingbirds–Juvenile literature.
Classification: LCC QL696.P25 A76 2018 | DDC 598.8'44–dc23

First Edition

Published in 2018 by
Gareth Stevens Publishing
111 East 14th Street, Suite 349
New York, NY 10003

Copyright © 2018 Gareth Stevens Publishing

Designer: Laura Bowen
Editor: Therese Shea

Photo credits: Cover, p. 1 (mockingbird) Steve Byland/Shutterstock.com; cover, pp. 1–32 (paper texture) javarman/Shutterstock.com; cover, pp. 1–32 (footprints) pio3/Shutterstock.com; pp. 4–29 (note paper) totallyPic.com/Shutterstock.com; pp. 4–29 (photo frame, tape) mtkang/Shutterstock.com; p. 5 (main) wavebreakmedia/Shutterstock.com; p. 5 (inset) Crisco/Shutterstock.com; p. 7 Tania Thomson/Shutterstock.com; pp. 9, 25 (bottom), 27 Chesapeake Images/Shutterstock.com; p. 11 Toni Ard/Moment/Getty Images; p. 13 (map) Ken Thomas/Wikimedia Commons; p. 13 (bird) Jill Nightingale/Shutterstock.com; p. 15 Bonnie Taylor Barry/Shutterstock.com; p. 17 cliff collings/Shutterstock.com; p. 19 Distinctive Images/Moment/Getty Images; p. 21 Angelo DeSantis/Moment Open/Getty Images; p. 23 CatbirdHill/Shutterstock.com; p. 25 (top) tdoes/Shutterstock.com; p. 29 Danita Delimont/Gallo Images/Getty Images.

Printed in the United States of America

CPSIA compliance information: Batch #CS17GS: For further information contact Gareth Stevens, New York, New York at 1-800-542-2595.

CONTENTS

Words in the glossary appear in **bold** type the first time they are used in the text.

WELCOME TO MY WORLD

This is my journal. Hopefully, I'll be the only one reading it. I'm hiding it from my brother and sister!

My plan is to become a wildlife **photographer**. I started this journal to improve my photography skills. I'm going to take pictures of birds. Right now, my bird **obsession** is mockingbirds. They're cool birds—and a little weird, too. I'll collect mockingbird facts and photos in this book, in case I need them in the future!

I'll be taking photos of the mockingbirds in my backyard. Maybe my photos will appear in a famous magazine or on a cool website someday!

THE NORTHERN MOCKINGBIRD

IT'S THE STATE BIRD OF:

Arkansas

Florida

Mississippi

Tennessee

Texas

The only species, or kind, of mockingbirds that live in North America are northern mockingbirds. This species is found all over the United States, in southern Canada, and in Mexico. They can even live in cities, as long as they can find food there!

Northern mockingbirds are a gray color with a light-colored belly. Mockingbirds can be as long as 10 inches (25 cm). Their wingspan can be as wide as 13 inches (33 cm) from tip to tip!

I caught this mockingbird spreading its wings!

7

AMAZING MEMORY

IN THE NAME

scientists' name for the northern mockingbird = Mimus polyglottos

Mimus = Latin for "mimic"

I love mockingbirds because of their singing. The first time I heard a mockingbird, I thought there were 10 different birds in the yard. I heard so many songs, but there was just one bird! Mockingbirds can mimic, or copy, the songs and calls of other birds.

One mockingbird can learn more than 30 songs from other birds. Some say they can learn more than 100 calls! They sing all day and sometimes at night, too.

This mockingbird is singing!

9

NOT JUST SONGS!

OLDEST MOCKINGBIRD

14 years, 10 months old

(I wonder how many songs and calls it knew!)

Learning and singing all those songs is pretty cool. I don't know that many songs myself! And mockingbirds don't just copy bird noises. I found this out when I was in the backyard throwing a ball to my dog Chuck. Chuck barked, and then I heard a bark behind me. I looked back, and there was a mockingbird "barking" like Chuck! I couldn't believe it!

I **researched** and found out that mockingbirds can make noises like lots of animals. They even mimic objects, such as car alarms!

Mockingbirds learn more and more songs throughout their lives. That's a bit like people!

CLOSE CALL

THE LOW LIFE

Mockingbird nests may be as low as 3 feet (0.9 m) off the ground.

Because mockingbirds had such a great trick, people in the 1800s caught them and put them in cages. They even took babies out of nests! So sad! They caught so many that mockingbirds almost disappeared in some places. Luckily, mockingbirds didn't die out. Laws were **enacted** that stopped "cagebird trade."

Now, mockingbirds are spreading. Some people think it's because more people are planting rosebushes where mockingbirds like to live. They also live in thick **hedges**.

Northern Mockingbird Range

North America

☐ summer
☐ all year

I'd hate to see the birds in my backyard in a cage!

13

TIME FOR A TASTE

THE MOCKINGBIRD DIET (No, Thanks!)

beetles, grasshoppers, moths, caterpillars, ants, wasps, spiders, snails, earthworms, and sometimes crayfish and small lizards

We have bird feeders in our backyard, but the mockingbirds don't seem very interested in the seeds we put in them. Instead, they walk or run along the ground, looking for bugs to eat. I've also seen them eating berries off the bushes.

I saw a mockingbird sitting still on a branch today. Then, it swooped down and picked up something from the ground. I'm guessing it was watching the grass for bugs to eat.

Mockingbirds eat more bugs in spring and summer. They eat more berries in fall and winter.

WEIRD MOVES!

It's Greek!

The Greek word *ornis* means "bird." That's where the word "ornithologist" comes from.

Today, I was watching a mockingbird in our backyard. It was doing something weird with its wings. It would open them and close them. I read it's called a "wing flash," and no one really knows why they do it.

People who study birds, called ornithologists, think they're showing off the white patches on their wings to scare bugs so they're easier to find. But it doesn't seem to work that well, so maybe that's not the reason?

Not all mockingbird species have the white patches on their wings, but the northern mockingbird does!

17

MOCKINGBIRD MATES

Full Moon Melody

Males without mates sing more than males with mates. They love to sing during a full moon!

It's hard to tell the difference between male and female mockingbirds. Males are a bit bigger. I'd have to see them next to each other to know which is which. Males sing louder than females, so that's another way to tell them apart. Males really sing a lot when they're looking for a **mate**. Sometimes a male mockingbird leaps in the air and flaps, too!

After the female mockingbird chooses a mate, the two make a nest. Then, the female lays two to six bluish or greenish eggs.

Mockingbirds usually mate between April and July. In this picture, the male must be the one singing!

19

BIRD ATTACK!

I saw something crazy today. A mockingbird was diving at the neighbor's cat, Mittens. The cat was so scared that he ran away!

I think the mockingbird was trying to **defend** its nest. I read that they get very **aggressive** when they're guarding their nests. Sometimes they even attack people who get too close! I'm not sure where the nest is, but I'm going to find out tomorrow. I'll sit quietly on the deck and watch the mockingbirds' movements.

Dangerous Song!

A mockingbird might sing a warning song before it attacks!

I was glad I had
my camera so I
could take a picture.
Poor Mittens!

21

THE NEST

Nests Are Made of:

- weeds
- grass
- leaves
- moss
- animal hair

I found the nest! I knew it wouldn't be too high up, so I looked low. Mockingbirds don't usually build their nest higher than 10 feet (3 m) from the ground. The one I found was only about 3 feet (0.9 m) high.

Mother mockingbirds sit on the eggs to keep them warm, but both mothers and fathers feed the birds. I see two birds darting back and forth from the nest, so the eggs must have **hatched**. The baby mockingbirds must be hungry!

Mockingbird nests are shaped like a cup.

FROM NESTLING TO FLEDGLING

Growing Up Mockingbird

- 2 weeks in their eggs
- 12 days in the nest after hatching
- 2 weeks of learning how to fly

Baby mockingbirds are called nestlings when they're first born. They stay in their nest for about 2 weeks, growing feathers and begging for food. Then, they leave for the first time to try to fly. It takes them about a week to get it right.

I've seen the babies, now called fledglings, fluttering around on the ground. They'd better learn how to fly soon or Mittens the cat will be back! The father teaches them—like how Dad taught me to ride a bike!

nestlings

I asked Mom to use her special camera lens to zoom in and take these photos.

fledgling and dad

GOOD-BYE, MOCKINGBIRDS!

Friend or Foe?

People think mockingbirds know the difference between friendly people and those who would harm them. I hope the mockingbirds in my yard know I'm friendly.

I don't see the young mockingbirds around anymore. They must have flown off. Wow, they grow up fast! They'll be able to have their own families in about a year. For now, at least they know how to find enough food to stay alive.

The mockingbird parents may mate again and have another brood, or family. They can have up to three broods a year. Mockingbirds usually live about 5 years, so they may have a lot of chicks!

Here's a mockingbird on our fence. It has feathers, but it doesn't look quite like an adult yet. I think it's a fledgling.

27

MARVELOUS MOCKINGBIRDS

Seasonal Singing

A male mockingbird may have two sets of songs: one for spring and one for fall!

Northern mockingbirds have a lot of berries to eat around here in winter, but it's too hard to find bugs to eat because of the frozen ground. Some mockingbirds **migrate** south in the winter, but not all. Some stick around all year. Northern mockingbird migration isn't really understood by scientists.

I'll watch through the winter and take notes in this journal. I might learn something that will help ornithologists understand this cool bird better! I'm getting good at bird-watching!

If I don't become a wildlife photographer, I'll be an ornithologist!

29

GLOSSARY

aggressive: showing a readiness to attack

defend: to keep something safe

enact: to make a bill become part of the law

hatch: to come out of an egg

hedge: a row of shrubs or small trees that are planted close to each other in order to form a boundary

mate: one of two animals that come together to make babies. To come together to make babies.

migrate: to move to warmer or colder places for a season

obsession: something that a person is very interested in and thinks about a lot

photographer: one who practices the art of taking pictures with a camera

research: to study to find something new

subject: someone or something being studied

FOR MORE INFORMATION

Books

Avery, Mark. *Remarkable Birds*. New York, NY: Thames & Hudson, 2016.

Sorenson, Sharon. *Birds in the Yard Month by Month*. Mechanicsburg, PA: Stackpole Books, 2013.

Websites

Northern Mockingbird
www.allaboutbirds.org/guide/Northern_Mockingbird/lifehistory
Check out some cool facts about the northern mockingbird.

Northern Mockingbird
www.audubon.org/field-guide/bird/northern-mockingbird
Read more about this cool species.

Types of Mockingbirds
animals.mom.me/types-mockingbirds-4790.html
Find out about the different species of mockingbirds.

INDEX